11 3X

WITHDRAWN

S0-ALI-188

CR

SHARKS SET II

SEAL SHARKS

Adam G. Klein
ABDO Publishing Company

3 1336 07220 2956

SAN DIEGO PUBLIC LIBRARY
CHILDREN'S ROOM

visit us at
www.abdopub.com

Published by ABDO Publishing Company, 4940 Viking Drive, Edina, Minnesota 55435.
Copyright © 2006 by Abdo Consulting Group, Inc. International copyrights reserved in all
countries. No part of this book may be reproduced in any form without written permission from the
publisher. The Checkerboard Library™ is a trademark and logo of ABDO Publishing Company.

Printed in the United States.

Cover Photo: © Rudie Kuiter / SeaPics.com
Interior Photos: © Andrew J. Martinez / SeaPics.com p. 10; Corbis pp. 8, 18; © Doug Perrine /
     SeaPics.com pp. 13, 15, 17; marinethemes.com/Kelvin Aitken pp. 5, 21; © Mark Conlin /
     SeaPics.com p. 19; © Michael S. Nolan / SeaPics.com p. 11; © Rudie Kuiter / SeaPics.com p. 9;
     Uko Gorter pp. 6-7

Series Coordinator: Heidi M. Dahmes
Editors: Heidi M. Dahmes, Megan M. Gunderson
Art Direction: Neil Klinepier

Library of Congress Cataloging-in-Publication Data

Klein, Adam G., 1976-
   Seal sharks / Adam G. Klein.
      p. cm. -- (Sharks. Set II)
   ISBN 1-59679-289-2
      1. Kitefin shark--Juvenile literature. I. Title.

QL638.95.D3K59 2005
597.3--dc22

                                                              2005048160

CONTENTS

Seal Sharks and Family

The ocean is a big place, and there is a lot to explore. There are more than 200 shark species. Sharks are fish that have skeletons made of **cartilage** rather than bone. They have two pairs of fins. And their skin is covered in **dermal denticles**, which act as a protective covering.

A seal shark cruises through the water to look for its next meal. It may come across an animal much bigger than itself. Normally, a creature would pass by without thinking of attacking the larger animal. But, the seal shark has a way of feasting on the largest creatures of the sea.

The seal shark is a fascinating animal. It lives deep in the ocean. The more people come in contact with these fish, the more they seem to learn. And, the more amazing seal sharks become.

Seal sharks are solitary animals.
They rarely travel in schools.

What They Look Like

Female seal sharks grow to be larger than males. Adult females can grow to 63 inches (160 cm) long. Males reach a maximum length of about 47 inches (120 cm).

Seal sharks have a slender trunk and a short, blunt snout. They have large, pale lips. Their upper teeth are slender and curve outward toward the corners of the mouth. Their lower teeth are straight and triangular.

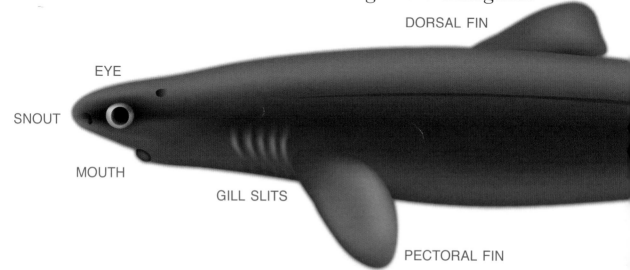

DORSAL FIN

EYE

SNOUT

MOUTH

GILL SLITS

PECTORAL FIN

Seal sharks are a gray or dark brown color. Sometimes, the back is covered with black spots. The tail is capped with black. And, the **dorsal** and **pectoral** fins have whitish edges.

A seal shark's body is made for ocean living. Its **liver** is about one-fifth of its body weight. The liver contains oil that makes the shark float naturally in the water. And, the seal shark's **cartilaginous** skeleton is lighter than bone.

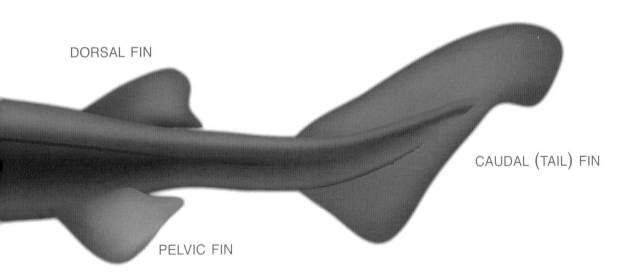

DORSAL FIN

CAUDAL (TAIL) FIN

PELVIC FIN

WHERE THEY LIVE

Seal sharks live near New Zealand, Australia, Japan, and the Hawaiian Islands. They swim through waters near the west coast of Africa up through Ireland. And, they live in the northern Gulf of Mexico as well as in the western areas of the Mediterranean Sea.

Seal sharks are deepwater fish. Typically they are found between 121 and 5,905 feet (37 and 1,800 m) deep. They are considered a bottom-dwelling species. But, they often live far above the ocean floor.

A variety of animals swim through Australia's coastal waters.

The seal shark is a deepwater shark. So, it is hard to study, and its population size is difficult to estimate.

Most sharks are cold-blooded. This means their body temperature depends on the surrounding water. So, sharks try to remain in places where they can maintain their body temperature and feel comfortable. The seal shark chooses warm or tropical water to live in.

FOOD

There is plenty to eat in the ocean's deeper areas. Seal sharks feast on **crustaceans**, squid, octopuses, and annelid worms. They also snack on a variety of bony fish and **elasmobranches**.

Larger creatures are not safe from the seal shark either. With its tiny upper teeth, a seal shark hooks on to its target's body. The seal shark's large lips are used to suction, or attach, itself to the animal.

There are many species of marine annelid worms. They come in various sizes and shapes. And, they make tasty treats for seal sharks!

Once attached, the seal shark spins around in a circle. The lower rigid teeth cut a ball-like piece of flesh from the larger creature. This unusual feeding method leaves the seal shark's prey alive, but scarred.

This dolphin was the victim of a cookie cutter shark attack. This bite is similar to the damage a seal shark would do.

SENSES

Deep underwater, a seal shark has to figure out what is above, below, and near it. Sharks can see, hear, taste, smell, and touch. But, they also have senses that humans cannot relate to. Their senses are specially adapted for their **environment**.

Sharks can hear low vibration noise through ears contained in sacs in their heads. They detect particles in the water, such as blood, through their noses. They also have the ability to sense electrical charges in the water, as well as changes in water pressure.

With these special senses, sharks are very aware of their surroundings. Sharks use all of their senses to locate food, to detect **predators**, and to find a mate.

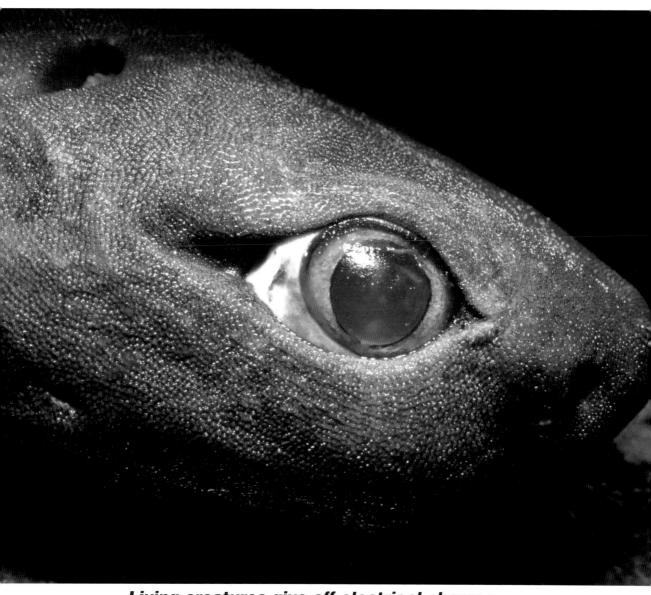

Living creatures give off electrical charges.
Sharks pick up these charges and know
that either a meal or a predator is nearby.

BABIES

Reproduction is important to the survival of shark species. It takes a long time for sharks to reach **maturity**. So, it is important for them to live long enough to reproduce.

Scientists are not sure at what age seal sharks become mature. Male seal sharks are ready to reproduce when they are between 32 and 47 inches (80 and 120 cm) long. Female seal sharks are mature when they reach 47 to 55 inches (120 to 140 cm) in length.

After an adult male and female mate, the baby sharks begin to develop. Seal sharks grow in eggs inside their mother. A yolk sac is attached to each **embryo**. This provides the nourishment the developing sharks need.

Baby sharks are called pups. Seal shark pups are birthed in **litters** of 10 to 16 young. They are typically around 12 inches (30 cm) long at birth.

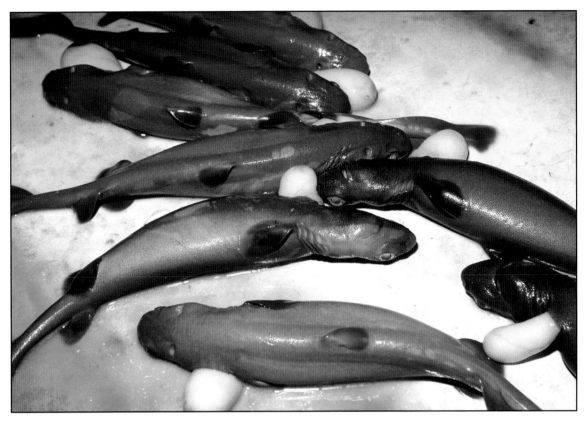

These seal sharks were discarded at a processing plant. Fishing for sharks is harmful to shark populations. If sharks cannot reproduce, the populations will not survive.

Seal shark pups are born fully developed and ready for the world. Still, the pups will have to be clever to survive. The mother swims away soon after her babies are born.

ATTACK AND DEFENSE

The seal shark is a powerful **predator**. Seal sharks attack creatures much larger than themselves. Using their teeth, they take perfect round plugs out of their victims. Fishers dislike seal sharks because this process can damage an entire catch.

A seal shark has no defense against humans. So, the seal shark's biggest threat is commercial fishing. A recent increase in deepwater fishing is reducing the seal shark's numbers. Currently, the seal shark is considered a near-threatened species.

Captured seal sharks are used in many products. The oil from their **livers** is used in cosmetics and machine oil. Their skin is made into leather. Seal shark leather is used for polishing cabinets and making jewelry. And, shark **cartilage** is used in health care products.

This seal shark is being processed at a fish plant. Continued fishing will put the seal shark population at risk of disappearing.

ATTACKS ON HUMANS

Sharks have received a bad reputation as being violent killers. But, sharks do not naturally prey on humans. Most people will never encounter a shark. And, seal sharks are not known to be harmful to humans.

Shark attacks occur for various reasons. Sharks attack as a form of defense when they feel threatened. After all, you might be seen as the invader of their world. So, swimmers should avoid approaching a shark.

Take heed of signs such as this one before entering the ocean!

18

Sharks may also attack when they are hungry. Sharks are usually on the lookout for food. When humans swim, their movements resemble those of a wounded animal. A hungry shark will pick up these vibrations and go to investigate.

Spearfishing increases the risk of attack. This catch could attract a hungry shark.

SEAL SHARK FACTS

Scientific Name:

Seal shark   *Dalatias licha*

Average Size:

Female seal sharks are typically larger than males.
Adult females can grow to 63 inches (160 cm) long.
Males reach a maximum length of about 47 inches
(120 cm).

Where They're Found:

Seal sharks live throughout the oceans of the world.

Seal sharks are also known
as kitefin sharks.

GLOSSARY

cartilage (KAHR-tuh-lihj) - the soft, elastic connective tissue in the skeleton. A person's nose and ears are made of cartilage.

crustacean (kruhs-TAY-shuhn) - any of a group of animals with hard shells that live mostly in water. Crabs, lobsters, and shrimps are all crustaceans.

dermal denticle - a small toothlike projection on a shark's skin.

dorsal - located near or on the back, especially of an animal.

elasmobranch (ih-LAZ-muh-branch) - any fish made of cartilage that has five to seven gill slits on each side, including sharks, skates, and rays.

embryo - an organism in the early stages of development.

environment - all the surroundings that affect the growth and well-being of a living thing.

litter - all of the pups born at one time to a mother shark.

liver - a large organ that produces bile, stores carbohydrates, and performs other bodily functions.

maturity - the state of having reached full growth or development.

pectoral - located in or on the chest.

predator - an animal that kills and eats other animals.

WEB SITES

To learn more about seal sharks, visit ABDO Publishing Company on the World Wide Web at **www.abdopub.com**. Web sites about seal sharks are featured on our Book Links page. These links are routinely monitored and updated to provide the most current information available.

INDEX